RSPB
Pocket Book of
Owls

RSPB
Pocket Book of
Owls

Marianne Taylor

BLOOMSBURY WILDLIFE
LONDON • OXFORD • NEW YORK • NEW DELHI • SYDNEY

The RSPB Pocket Book series invites readers to explore the deeper and wilder worlds of some of our most familiar and beloved wild species. We take a deep but undaunting dive into their lives and ways, their evolution and anatomy, and their resonance and value to us in our own lives, from our earliest depictions of their form to the ways that we are working to safeguard them and their habitats for the future.

The *RSPB Pocket Book of Owls* introduces these enigmatic birds as we know them – and as we think we know them – revealing the secrets of their lives under cover of darkness. To understand owls is to understand how they evolved and adapted to a highly specialised way of life: through supersenses, steely stomachs, and feathers as soft as their talons are deadly. To understand how people relate to owls is to explore how we have painted, carved and written about these birds from the earliest times to the present day. Along the way, there are surprises – ultraviolet fluorescence, serpentine housekeepers, and a twelfth-century rap battle all make appearances. The book is richly illustrated with line drawings of owls from the British Isles and beyond.

Marianne Taylor is a nature and wildlife writer and illustrator who loves owls. Her previous books include *RSPB British Birds of Prey*, *Beautiful Owls*, and *Owls: a guide to every species in the world*.

The RSPB is the UK's largest conservation charity, protecting habitats, saving species, and helping to end the climate and nature emergency. By buying this book, you are helping to fund the RSPB's conservation work. If you would like to know more about the RSPB, visit their website at www.rspb.org.uk or write to: The RSPB, The Lodge, Sandy, Bedfordshire, SG19 2DL.

Bloomsbury Wildlife is the proud home of many of the best and most passionate nature writers around. With books on everything from mushrooms to marine animals and ducks to dinosaurs, readers of all levels and interests are sure to find something engaging among our extensive range of natural history titles.

BLOOMSBURY WILDLIFE
Bloomsbury Publishing Plc
50 Bedford Square, London, WC1B 3DP, UK
Bloomsbury Publishing Ireland Limited,
29 Earlsfort Terrace, Dublin 2, Ireland

BLOOMSBURY, BLOOMSBURY WILDLIFE and the Diana logo
are trademarks of Bloomsbury Publishing Plc

First published in the United Kingdom 2026

A catalogue record for this book is available from the British Library
Library of Congress Cataloguing-in-Publication data has been applied for

ISBN: HB: 978-1-3994-2875-0; ePub: 978-1-3994-2874-3

2 4 6 8 10 9 7 5 3 1

Design by Austin Taylor
Printed and bound in Great Britain by Clays Ltd, Elcograf S.p.A.

MIX
Paper | Supporting
responsible forestry
FSC® C018072
www.fsc.org

To find out more about our authors and books, visit www.bloomsbury.com
and sign up for our newsletters
For product-safety-related questions, contact productsafety@bloomsbury.com

Published under licence from RSPB Sales Limited to raise awareness of the RSPB
(charity registration in England and Wales no 207076 and Scotland no SC037654)

For all licensed products sold by Bloomsbury Publishing Limited, Bloomsbury
Publishing Limited will donate a minimum of 2% from all sales to RSPB Sales Ltd,
which gives all its distributable profits through Gift Aid to the RSPB

Contents

CHAPTER ONE

Introducing Owls

People have always felt a special connection with owls. Across centuries and cultures, their image has appeared in art, myth and story – their forward-facing eyes and expressive faces echo our own, seeming almost more human than bird. Yet despite this familiarity, living owls remain elusive. Their nocturnal habits, secretive behaviour and otherworldly senses make them difficult to see and harder still to truly know.

It's no wonder our responses to owls are so complex. In some traditions, these mysterious birds are feared, in others revered. Folklore casts them as omens of fortune or death; fiction embodies them with the guiding wisdom of nature itself.

But owls are more than symbols. They are ecologically vital as predators that interact with a host of other species, shaping the balance of their habitats – and they are widely misunderstood. Today, science is helping us replace mystery with insight, revealing the rich, layered lives of these superbly adapted birds. And the more we learn, the more remarkable they become.

What is an owl?

The owls form a very distinctive group of predatory birds. You will recognise one immediately by its flat facial disc. Owls also have soft camouflaged plumage, mainly nocturnal habits, and taloned feet with two toes pointing forwards and two backwards. They form a taxonomic grouping of birds known as an order – one of 44 orders of birds in the world. The name of this order is Strigiformes – derived from *strix*, a Greek word for owl. Owls are categorised as birds of prey, along with two other orders – Accipitriformes (hawks, eagles, kites and harriers) and Falconiformes (falcons and caracaras). The last two groups are also known as the raptors, or the diurnal birds of prey. 'Diurnal' means 'active in the daytime', so they are different from typical nocturnal owls in this respect.

Owls of the world

Worldwide, there are more than 250 different species of owls, found across six continents. The familiar image of an owl – a medium-sized bird, deep in woodland, hunting small furry mammals at night and resting in a favourite hiding perch by day – fits many species, but not all. Some owls are barely

Eurasian
Pygmy Owl

Eurasian Eagle-owl

Burrowing Owl

sparrow-sized and feed on insects, while the largest eagle-owls are powerful apex predators, capable of taking prey as large as deer fawns and herons.

Not all owls are nocturnal, and not all live in forests. Some thrive in open grasslands or tundra, and a few species are restless travellers. Some regularly migrate every year over varying distances – in some cases covering thousands of kilometres. Others are nomadic, roaming around in varying directions whenever they need to, in response to food availability and changing conditions.

Barn Owl

Marsh Owl

OWLS IN NUMBERS

....

Biggest, fastest, wisest...? The world's record-breaking owl species are a very varied bunch.

Largest – Blakiston's Fish Owl and the Eurasian Eagle-owl can both be 70–75cm tall and weigh up to 4.6kg. The Great Grey Owl has a long tail and can top 80cm in total length, but weighs much less – a maximum of about 1.9kg.

Smallest – The Elf Owl stands only 13.5cm tall and weighs about 40g.

Rarest – The Siau Scops Owl may already be extinct, with only a handful of unconfirmed sightings since its discovery in 1866. The Pernambuco Pygmy Owl is in a similar position – the last confirmed sighting was in 2001.

Most widespread – The Short-eared Owl is found across North America and Eurasia, as well as large parts of South America, a few parts of Africa, and various isolated island groups.

Fastest – This may be the Great Horned Owl, with a top speed of nearly 65km/h. Although the flight speed of many other owls is not known, the Great Horned is a very large and powerful owl that is adapted to travel quickly over open spaces, so is likely to outpace smaller species that live in more restricted habitats.

Wisest – Despite their reputation, owls are not the cleverest or biggest-brained birds – but nor are they unintelligent. Predators must outwit prey so are generally quite clever. Social species also tend to show higher intelligence, which may make the Burrowing Owl – the most social owl – the brainiest. But until all owl species take an avian IQ test, this remains speculation. Whether any owl could outwit the bird world's real big-brains, though, such as ravens and parrots, is doubtful.

Short-eared Owl

Barn Owl

Long-eared Owl

Tawny Owl

Little Owl

Owls of the British Isles

Of all the owl species found around the world, only five are resident and established breeding birds in the British Isles: the Tawny Owl, the Barn Owl, the Little Owl, the Long-eared Owl and the Short-eared Owl. Two other species have bred here but only in unusual or limited circumstances – a pair of Snowy Owls nested in Shetland for several years between 1967 and 1975, and a few wild-living Eurasian Eagle-owls, likely escapees from captivity, have also bred. Three more species are recorded as rare visitors, having arrived naturally from mainland Europe where they breed: Tengmalm's Owl, Northern Hawk Owl and Eurasian Scops Owl.

Why so few owls? One reason is that most species are not natural explorers. Around the world, many owls live only on a single island, even when other suitable habitats lie just across the water. In the British Isles, three of five resident species are among the more adventurous types of owl, while the Little Owl was introduced from mainland Europe by humans. The Tawny Owl is famously sedentary – so much so that it's one of the few birds found in Great Britain but not in Ireland. This absence gives Long-eared Owls a better chance in Ireland, where they aren't outcompeted by Tawnies for prime woodland habitat.

SPOTTING OWLS:
TIPS FOR OWL-WATCHERS

....

Each of the five resident owl species of the British Isles has its own preferred habitat and behaviour, which we'll explore later in the book. But here are a few general tips to help improve your chances of seeing one in the wild.

Time of day – Evenings are usually best – even the most daytime-active owls tend to be more active later in the day. Rain and wind can make hunting harder, so owls are often more active after a spell of bad weather has passed. Spring is a busy time for courtship, and midsummer sees adults hunting intensively to feed their chicks. On warm late-summer afternoons, you might also spot an owl sunbathing in the open.

Where to look – Try woodland edges, especially where patches of rough grassland are nearby. Mature trees and old farm buildings can offer nesting and roosting sites.

Keep listening – Learning owl calls can help you locate them. You can find recordings online, for example on the RSPB's pages for each owl species (via the 'Bird A–Z' page). Owls are most vocal in late winter and early spring, and in summer you may hear young owls calling for food from their parents.

Respect their space – Avoid approaching nesting or resting sites. Use binoculars to watch from a distance. Binoculars with large objective lenses gather more light, giving you a brighter image than the naked eye – especially useful in low light. Using a spotting scope on a tripod can be more comfortable than binoculars if you are watching for a long time.

Owls and people

We humans tend to relate most strongly to animals that resemble us – especially those with forward-facing eyes and expressive faces. Owls are the most human-like of birds in appearance, and it's easy to caricature an owl's face to look comically expressive while keeping it recognisably owl-like. In fact, many owls naturally seem to wear distinct expressions: the Little Owl's sternly disapproving frown, Tengmalm's Owl with its wide eyes and dark 'eyebrows' raised in surprise, or the Ural Owl's gentle gaze, which belies a temperament that's anything but gentle.

Yet despite the kinship we recognise in their faces, owls live very different lives from ours. We are sociable, daylight-loving beings; most owls are solitary, secretive and nocturnal. Perhaps that's why they've come to symbolise wisdom, mystery, and sometimes menace. Their image has appeared in art and storytelling since prehistory, linked to gods and witches, wizards and wild places, from forest to tundra.

Real owls also have a place in human history. In falconry, larger owl species have been trained to hunt gamebirds and rabbits for their owners, though they've never been as popular or as easily trained as hawks and falcons. For many people, falconry displays offer the only chance to see an owl up

An alert Eurasian Scops Owl,
ready to hunt, widens its eyes and
flattens its ear-tufts.

When it prepares to rest and
sleep, its face changes completely.

close – though there is growing concern about using nocturnal species in daytime falconry exhibitions.

In northern regions, some owls, such as the majestic Snowy Owl, are known as 'irruptive' migrants, appearing suddenly during harsh winters when they leave their usual territories in search of better hunting grounds. Their arrival often sparks fascination. And for birdwatchers, owls carry a particular magic: encounters are unpredictable, and usually happen in the quiet, shadowy hours of dawn or dusk. What better way to end a summer's day than to glimpse a Barn Owl drifting over a meadow in the last golden beams of sunlight?

Owls and ecology

All animals interact with others in some way – they may eat them, be eaten by them, or compete with them for food and space. Some are parasites, others hosts (and some are both!). Many species rely on others to shape the habitat they share, and some form close behavioural relationships that benefit one or both. Every animal also interacts with plants, fungi and microbes. Extend this web of connections outwards, and you have an ecosystem – a living network in which every species plays a role, and where one change can ripple through many other species, causing a cascade of widespread changes.

Owls, as predators, sit near the top of this web. Their survival depends on the plants and other organisms that convert sunlight into energy, and on the animals that feed on those plants – as well as the animals that feed on those animals. This layered reliance makes owls vulnerable: if prey populations decline, owl numbers will follow. A certain level of prey availability is essential for their survival.

AN OWL'S FOOD WEB

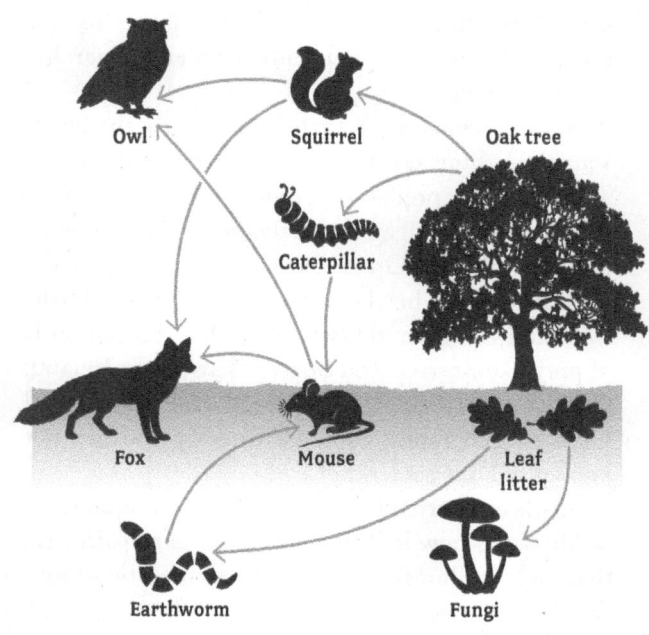

Fortunately, owls are adaptable. Species that hunt a wide variety of prey can cope when their favourites are scarce. And when prey is abundant, owls may breed more successfully, producing more chicks and allowing their populations to build up quickly. While predators can have short-term impacts on prey numbers, it's usually prey availability that determines populations of predators over time.

Owls themselves have few natural enemies, though smaller species are sometimes hunted by larger predators – including other owls. Their droppings and remains also contribute to the ecosystem, providing nutrients for plants, microbes and scavengers.

It may come as a surprise to learn that owls sometimes hunt other owls. This behaviour, known as 'intraguild predation', allows larger species to gain both a meal and an advantage by removing a competitor. In Great Britain, the Tawny is the biggest owl and has been known to prey on Little, Barn and Long-eared Owls, as well as diurnal birds of prey like Kestrels and Sparrowhawks. (In Ireland, there are only Barn, Long-eared and Short-eared Owls, which rarely compete directly and are not known to hunt each other.)

Owls are perfectly adapted to their unique ways of life. Let's now look at the evolutionary pathways that, over millions of years, have shaped them into the top-tier predators that they are today.

KEYSTONE SPECIES

In architecture, a *keystone* is the central, wedge-shaped stone at the top of an arch. It holds everything in place – without it, the arch would collapse. In nature, a *keystone species* plays a similar role. It helps to hold an entire ecosystem together, supporting and stabilising it, and if it disappears, many other species can be affected in surprising and far-reaching ways.

Some owls may be considered keystone species. The Ural Owl, a large bird found in Eurasian forests, is one example. It helps maintain balance among other birds of prey in the same habitat. By keeping numbers of medium-sized owls like the Tawny Owl in check, the Ural Owl indirectly protects smaller species such as Tengmalm's Owl, which might otherwise be outcompeted or preyed upon.

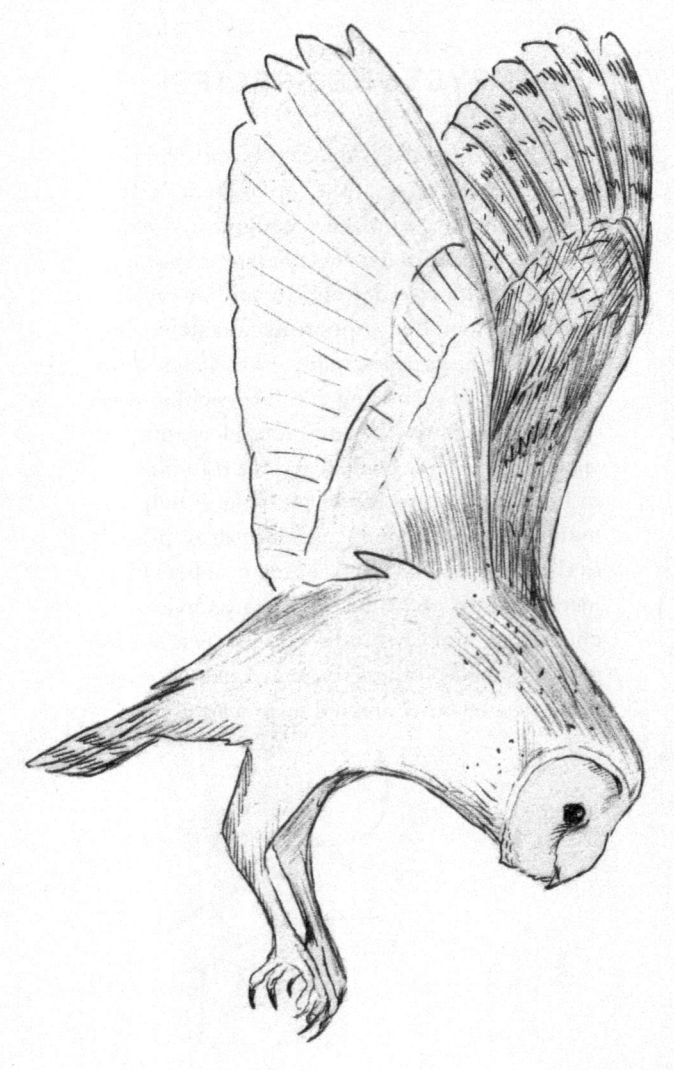

CHAPTER TWO

From Dinosaurs to Barn Owls

All wild animals are shaped by evolution – their bodies and behaviours finely tuned to the demands of survival. For owls, that means mastering the art of the hunt. To feed themselves and raise young, they must locate, catch and consume prey that is often alert, agile and determined not to be eaten. The result is a remarkable suite of adaptations: silent flight, extraordinary hearing and precision vision, all evolved for life in the dark.

Among birds, owls are unique. They share traits with other hunters – hawks and falcons, for example, also use powerful talons to capture and carry prey. However, while often grouped together with these groups as 'birds of prey', owls have taken a different evolutionary path. Nightjars and frogmouths seem very owl-like, being nocturnal and well camouflaged, but these similarities are superficial. Evolution does not always follow a straight line, and resemblance doesn't always mean relation.

To understand owls is to understand how evolution can shape an animal into something truly specialised – not only a bird of prey, but also a predator built for silence, stealth and surprise.

Earliest origins

Birds – including owls – are part of a remarkable evolutionary story that begins with dinosaurs. They evolved within a group of dinosaurs called theropods, some of which are familiar to us from books and films as this group includes famous names like *Velociraptor*, *Allosaurus* and *Tyrannosaurus*. These ancient animals walked on their hind legs and were carnivores (they ate other animals, rather than plants). In modern birds, the front legs are now wings, and the majority of species are still carnivores.

The first birds that we'd recognise today lived during the Cretaceous period (between 143 and 66 million years ago), sharing the world with other non-avian dinosaurs. They looked different from modern birds – with teeth in their jaws and claws on their wings – but fossils show they were unmistakably bird-like: feathered, warm-blooded, intelligent, and capable of flight. They hunted for food and cared for their eggs, just as birds still do.

When a giant asteroid struck Earth 66 million years ago, it wiped out most, but not all the dinosaurs. Birds were the only dinosaur group to survive the mass extinction. As the planet slowly recovered, these survivors spread across the globe, and evolved into the many kinds of birds we know today. Owls appeared early in this story: the oldest-known owl fossil is around 60 million years old, making the owls one of the earliest bird families that is still around today.

Fossils give us fascinating glimpses into the ancient history of owls. Long ago, owls were more varied than they are today, and among them were many species that hunted by day. Between 60 and

WHAT'S IN A NAME?

Birds often go by different names depending on where you are in the world, and sometimes they even have different common names within the same country. In the UK, for instance, the Barn Owl is occasionally called the screech owl, thanks to its eerie call.

To avoid confusion, scientists use a universal naming system to give each species a scientific name that also indicates its relationships to other species. Every bird has a scientific name made up of two parts: the genus (like a surname shared with close relatives) followed by its specific name (like a given name).

For example, all eared owls have the 'surname' *Asio* followed by their unique given names.

30 million years ago, several distinct owl families evolved, but many of them eventually became extinct. Hawks, it seems, were better suited to daytime hunting, and over time only the owls that specialised in night-time life survived to modern times. Today, a few owls are day-hunters, and a couple of hawk species also hunt mainly at dusk.

The Long-eared Owl is called *Asio otus*, and its close cousin the Short-eared Owl is *Asio flammeus*. Both belong to the genus *Asio*, which groups together closely related owls with similar features – in this case, ear tufts and long wings.

Altogether there are around 230 or so species in the typical owl family Strigidae, spread across about 23 genera. The barn owl family, Tytonidae, has fewer species, only 20 or so, grouped into two genera.

These scientific names aren't just labels; they're clues to evolutionary relationships, helping ornithologists trace how species are connected across the wider bird family tree. This is one reason we call them 'scientific' rather than 'Latin' names. Another is that their words aren't always Latin – *Tyto*, for example, comes from Ancient Greek.

Genetic history

By comparing owl DNA with that of other birds, scientists have discovered some surprising family ties. Owls are most closely related to hawks, and to a colourful group of birds that includes kingfishers,

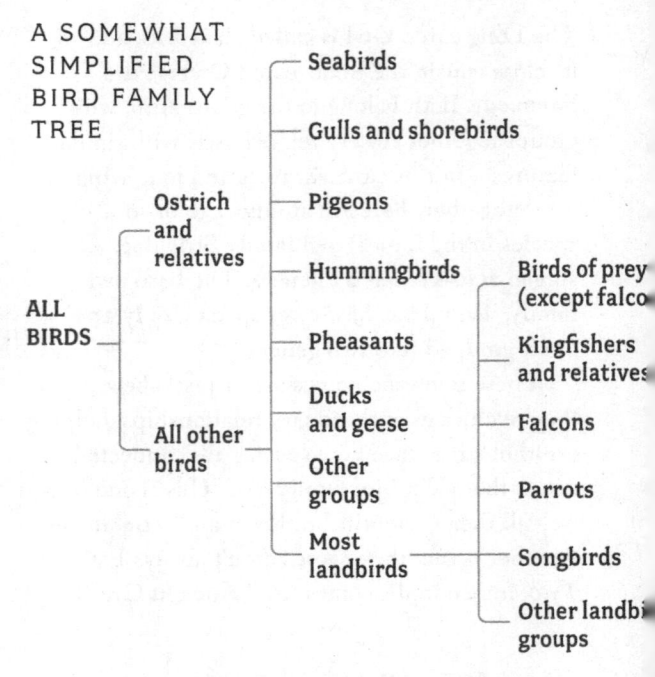

A SOMEWHAT SIMPLIFIED BIRD FAMILY TREE

ALL BIRDS
- Ostrich and relatives
- All other birds
  - Seabirds
  - Gulls and shorebirds
  - Pigeons
  - Hummingbirds
  - Pheasants
  - Ducks and geese
  - Other groups
  - Most landbirds
    - Birds of prey (except falco
    - Kingfishers and relatives
    - Falcons
    - Parrots
    - Songbirds
    - Other landb groups

hornbills and woodpeckers. Today, all owls fall into two broad families: Tytonidae and Strigidae. Tytonidae includes the barn and bay owls, while Strigidae encompasses the rest – the so-called 'typical owls'.

Studying owl DNA also helps scientists understand how different owl species are related.

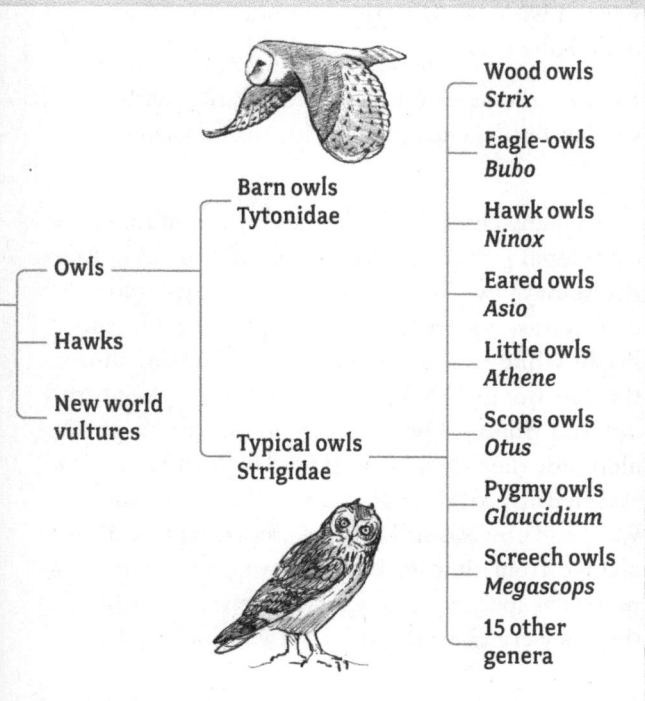

- Owls
- Hawks
- New world vultures

Barn owls
Tytonidae

Typical owls
Strigidae

Wood owls
Strix

Eagle-owls
Bubo

Hawk owls
Ninox

Eared owls
Asio

Little owls
Athene

Scops owls
Otus

Pygmy owls
Glaucidium

Screech owls
Megascops

15 other genera

Traditionally, owls have been grouped into categories called genera (singular: genus) based on how they look and behave. For example:

Strix – the wood owls, which live in forests and have short broad wings and large round heads.

Bubo – the eagle-owls, very large and powerful birds with striking ear tufts.

Asio – the eared owls, medium-sized and long-winged with ear tufts, they are often found in open habitats.

Ninox – the hawk owls, long-tailed owls with smaller heads, mostly found in Australasia.

In many cases, DNA studies have confirmed the traditional groupings of owls, but not always. Take the Snowy Owl, for example. It was once placed in its own genus, *Nyctea*, because of its unusual features: bright white feathers and a habit of hunting during the day. But its DNA tells a different story – it turns out the Snowy Owl belongs in the *Bubo* genus, alongside the Great Horned Owl of North America. As scientists continue to study bird genetics, the way we classify owls is still evolving, and scientific names change from time to time. If two populations of a particular species prove to be very genetically distinct, they may even be reclassified as two 'new' species.

Supersenses

Owls have some of the most distinctive faces in the animal kingdom – flat and rounded with big, forward-facing eyes, and often those striking feather tufts that look like ears. Their eyes may grab our attention, but evolution has shaped owls' faces to serve a different purpose – to enhance their hearing, which is the real star of their supersenses.

ORNAMENTAL EARS

The ear-like tufts of feathers on some owls'
heads give them a dramatic, expressive look,
not unlike a lynx. But these aren't ears at all,
just decorative plumage several centimetres
above their inconspicuous real ears.

So what are the tufts for? The most likely
explanation is camouflage. The tufts break up
the shape of the owl's head, helping it to look
like an angular broken branch, rather than
a living bird. These feather 'ears' are found
in several owl groups, from tiny scops and
screech owls to the powerful eagle-owls.

Unlike many mammals, which sniff out their prey, owls rely on a powerful combination of sight and sound – and in many species, sound is much more important. As in all birds, owls' ear openings are on the sides of their head, hidden beneath and protected by feathers. In many owls, one ear is set slightly higher than the other. This clever asymmetry means they can pinpoint exactly where a sound is coming from, even if it's directly above or below them.

The stiff little feathers that form the owl's facial disc act like a satellite dish, collecting and directing sound to the ears. Some owls even have a flap of skin (called an operculum) over the ear, which helps fine-tune the sound, filtering and focusing it. In the most nocturnal species, these adaptations have evolved to be so advanced that the owl can catch prey in pitch darkness, guided by sound alone.

Owls' eyes are also extraordinary. Like many night-time hunters, they have very large eyes for their body size – which means more light can reach the retina, the part of the eye that senses light, shade and colour, and sends this information to the brain. Their retinas are packed with rod cells, which are excellent at picking up contrast and detail and discerning movement in low light. They don't have many colour-detecting cone cells, though, so they don't see colour very well.

Owls' eyeballs are not round like ours – they're tube-shaped, which allows for a bigger retina but limits how much the eye can move in its socket. To make up for this, owls have very flexible necks and can turn their heads much further than we can – about 270 degrees (though not a full 360 – that famous 'fact' is a myth!). They also bob and tilt their heads rapidly when focusing on something, helping them judge distance and depth.

Their unusual eye anatomy means owls are a bit short-sighted. When they're up close – feeding their chicks, for example – they rely more on touch. Around the bill are fine whisker-like feathers called filoplumes, which help them feel what they're doing.

Stealthy killers

To be a successful hunter, an owl needs to hear its prey, while not being heard. Its feathers are specially adapted for silent flight. The leading edges of the flight feathers have tiny comb-like baffles that break up the air, muffling the sound of each wingbeat for a ninja-like approach. The result? A ghostly, gliding flight that's almost completely silent.

Many owls hunt animals that are moving through long grass, or even hidden under snow. Their long legs help them reach through the cover to grab their prey. Some smaller owls, especially those that eat insects, hover in front of trees and snatch prey straight from the leaves.

Most owls have broad, rounded wings, which make them agile in the air, though not especially fast. Many owls hunt from a perch, waiting and listening for prey before swooping down. Owls that hunt in open landscapes have longer, narrower wings, which help them fly further with less effort.

Owl feet are just as specialised. They have four toes, two pointing forwards and two backwards, an arrangement known as zygodactyl. It's unusual in birds, but gives owls a strong grip, which is especially useful when perching or grabbing prey. Some owls can even run across the ground to catch food – the Little Owl, for instance, is known to chase down insects and small mammals on foot.

Most owls also have feathered feet, which helps keep them warm, softens the sound of their landing, and protects them from bites or scratches. Like the filoplumes around the bill, these feathers also help them to feel what they are holding – useful when your dinner is trying to wriggle free.

Camouflage

Owls are masters of disguise. Four of the five species found in the British Isles wear mottled feathers in shades of grey and brown, helping them blend into tree bark, rocks and undergrowth. This clever camouflage allows them to rest in plain sight without being noticed.

The Barn Owl is the exception – with its pale gold, white and grey plumage, it stands out more easily. But it avoids detection by roosting in hidden places like tree hollows and old buildings.

Around the world, owls have evolved plumage to match their surroundings. In dense rainforest, some species are almost black, like the striking Black-banded Owl of South America. In snowy landscapes, the Snowy Owl wears a coat of white. Owls that live in deciduous woods tend to be browner, while those in pine forests are greyer with white speckles.

Some species, including the Tawny Owl and the Eastern and Western Screech Owls of North America, come in different colour forms, such as brown, grey or reddish brown, each suited to a particular habitat.

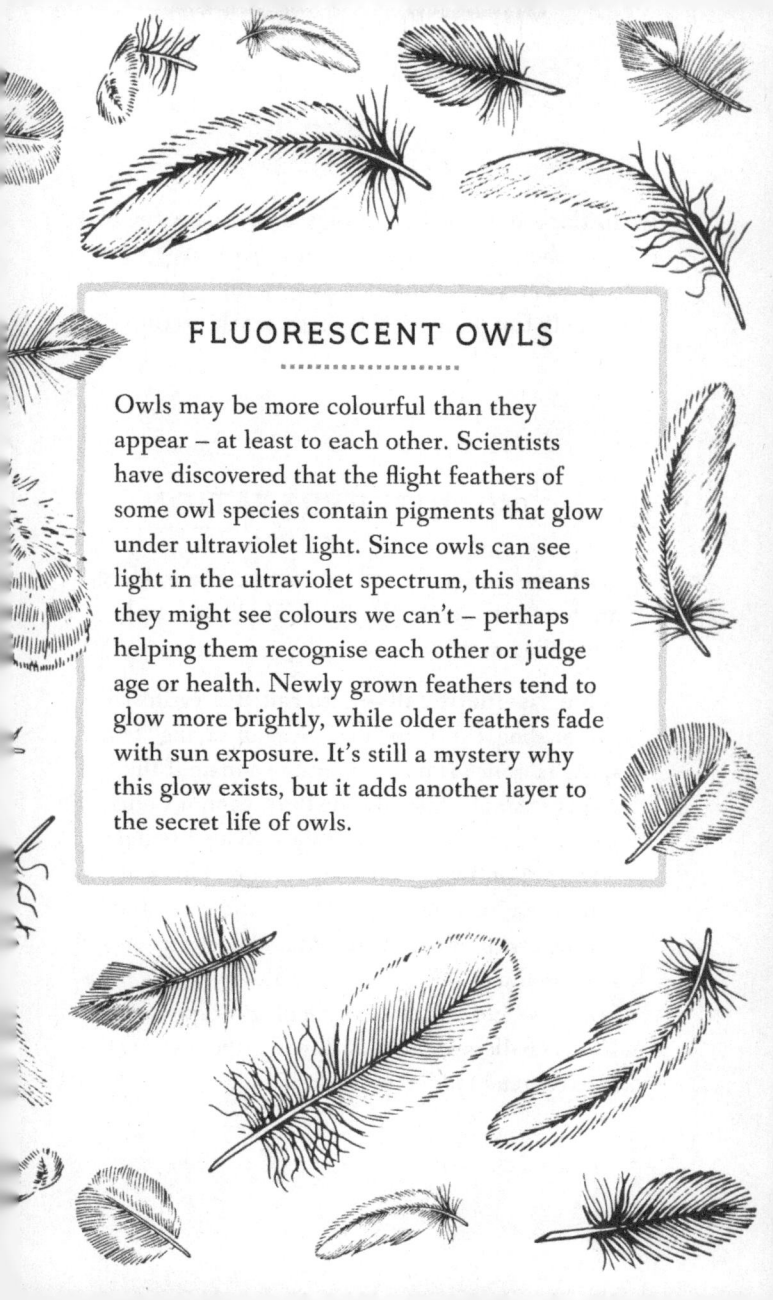

FLUORESCENT OWLS

Owls may be more colourful than they appear – at least to each other. Scientists have discovered that the flight feathers of some owl species contain pigments that glow under ultraviolet light. Since owls can see light in the ultraviolet spectrum, this means they might see colours we can't – perhaps helping them recognise each other or judge age or health. Newly grown feathers tend to glow more brightly, while older feathers fade with sun exposure. It's still a mystery why this glow exists, but it adds another layer to the secret life of owls.

Voice

In the dark, when visual signals aren't so useful, owls rely on their voices. And what voices they have — loud, far-carrying, and often surprisingly persistent. Owls call for many reasons: to mark territory, to

OWL INTERPRETATION

Owls use a range of calls to communicate. Here are four common types you might hear — and what they mean.

Advertisement call – Also called a territorial call or song, this is the owl's way of saying '*This space is mine*'. It may also invite a mate if the singer is single. Usually the most complex and persistent call is given by males, though females often join in with their own version. This call can take a lot of energy to make, and often the calling owl puffs up its throat and cocks up its tail as it produces the sound. The Tawny Owl's fluty '*whooooo*' hoot is an example of this type of call. If it is challenging a rival directly, the owl's call may become louder and faster.

find a mate, to stay in touch with a partner, or to warn of danger. Each owl has its own voice, and can recognise others by sound alone – not only what's being said, but also who is saying it.

Bigger owl species tend to have deeper voices, although within the same species the females usually sound higher-pitched, even though they are

Contact call – A short call meaning '*I'm here*'. Used between bonded pairs to check in or announce arrival. It can be soft or loud, depending on how far apart the owls are.

Begging call – Given by chicks to ask for food. Adult females may also use a version of this when they need their mate to bring a meal while they're busy with the nest.

Alarm call – A sharp, urgent version of the contact call that warns of danger. If a predator gets too close, owls may also hiss like a snake or snap their bills loudly to scare it off.

Owls have a lot to say, and a lot of different ways to say it. Learn how the five owl species in the British Isles use these sounds in the mini field guide on pages 120–122.

often slightly larger than their male counterparts. Barn Owls are known for their eerie screeches, while typical owls (such as Tawny, Long-eared, Short-eared and Little Owls) are more likely to hoot, bark or whistle. Some small species even sound like dripping water or chirping songbirds.

Owl calls are so distinctive that they are often the best way to tell species apart, especially in dense forests where the birds themselves are hard to spot. In fact, many new owl species have been discovered in recent decades by sound alone.

TO-WHIT, TO-WHO?
....

It is often said that the Tawny Owl calls '*to-whit, to-whooo*', and that this is a duet between a female (*to-whit*) and a male (*to-whooo*). That's partly true, but it's not the whole story.

Both male and female Tawny Owls can make both sounds, and they don't always sing to each other. The *to-whit* (or *ke-vick*) is a contact call, used in many situations. The *to-whooo* is the advertisement call, usually given by a territory-holding male – though females have their own version, which is wilder and shriller than the male's mellow, fluting call.

So next time you hear a Tawny Owl in the night, you might be listening to a solo, a duet, or something in between.

We hear owls calling at night, but what else do they get up to in the darkness? The next chapter takes a look at all the different activities that occupy owls during their waking hours.

CHAPTER THREE

A Day, Month and Year in the Life of Owls

As we go about our daily
routines, most owls are resting.
Their activity begins as ours winds down
– a life lived largely in darkness, shaped
by moonlight, silence, and the movements
of nocturnal prey. But not all owls follow
the same schedule. Most stir at dusk, but a
few hunt in daylight, and these patterns
may shift with the seasons, the weather,
and the demands of survival.

Unlike its daily rhythms, an owl's yearly cycle aligns more closely with that of other birds. Breeding takes place when food is most abundant. After young owls leave the nest and become independent, they may quickly have to leave their parents' territory and look for one of their own. For some species, the end of the breeding season means long-distance travel for both the adults and the youngsters, seeking out more favourable conditions or richer feeding grounds. Winter, for many, is a time of endurance – conserving energy, staying warm, and waiting for the lean season to pass – but courtship activity may begin well before the winter weather has passed.

To understand owls, we must look not only at how they live, but also *when* – across hours, months and years, through cycles of activity, rest and renewal.

Roamers and stay-at-homers

Owls in the British Isles live very different kinds of lives to each other – and two species show just how varied their routines can be. The Short-eared Owl is a wanderer, travelling long distances over the course of a year in search of food and nesting sites. It's flexible about where and when it breeds, adapting to changing conditions.

The Tawny Owl, on the other hand, is a true homebody. Once it finds a good territory as a youngster, it will stay there for life – year in, year out, through all seasons. By the age of three or four, a Tawny is ready to breed. It will already know its Tawny neighbours and may attract a mate to its patch, or move into a nearby territory held by a single neighbour of the opposite sex.

Once paired, Tawny Owls stick to a familiar routine: defending their territory, nesting in the same spot each year, and following a regular timetable for breeding.

Other owls of the British Isles fall somewhere in between. The Little Owl is also quite settled, while Barn Owls and Long-eared Owls prefer to hold a year-round territory but will move on if they need to. These lifestyle differences are closely linked to what each species eats and how it hunts – something we'll explore in chapter 4.

THE TAWNY OWL'S YEAR

January

Defending
territory is top
priority. If unpaired,
it's time to start
looking for a mate.

February

Much the same
as January. Pairs
begin bonding and
preparing a nest
site.

May

Parents feed
and protect their
growing chicks.

June

Young owls
leave the nest but
still rely on their
parents.

September

Adults defend
their territory from
wandering young
owls.

October

Still defending
territory. Many
young owls are still
searching for a territory
of their own.

March	April
March	**April**
Eggs are laid around mid-month.	Incubation begins. Males bring food for the females, who stay on the nest. Chicks hatch from mid-April.
July	**August**
Chicks begin to fend for themselves. They and their parents start moulting.	Young owls disperse or are pushed out by parents. Moulting continues.
November	**December**
Unpaired adults start trying to attract a mate. Young owls without a territory face a tough time.	Focus shifts to survival: keeping warm, holding on to territory and, for Tawnies that are still unpaired, attracting a mate.

Sleep and wake

Owls don't all follow the same schedule. Some are creatures of the night, others are active in daylight. The Long-eared Owl and Tawny Owl are our most nocturnal species, often not active at all until full darkness falls. Short-eared Owls and Little Owls are more flexible and are often active in daylight, especially in the late afternoon. The Barn Owl mainly hunts at night. However, because it hunts on the wing and in the open, and relies on its hearing to find prey, it can struggle in heavy rain or windy conditions. If a Barn Owl has poor hunting success overnight because of this, it might have to make an earlier start the following day when the weather breaks, and head out before nightfall.

The Tawny Owl, which hunts mainly in sheltered woodland, is less affected by bad weather. However, young Tawny Owls that are really struggling to survive may have to hunt by day.

Because most owls sleep during the day – when other birds are awake – they need to hide. If spotted, they risk being mobbed by smaller birds that see them as a threat. Some owls are even vulnerable to larger daytime predators like Goshawks or eagles.

That's why daytime roosts are carefully chosen. Owls that stay in one place year-round often sleep in or near their nesting site. More nomadic species

BIRDS OF A FEATHER

We often think of owls as solitary, only seeking company during the breeding season. But some species are more sociable than we might expect.

Outside of breeding, owls that aren't strongly territorial may sleep near others of their kind in communal roosts. In the British Isles, Long-eared Owls often roost in small groups in winter (see illustration on page 54). On mainland Europe, some winter roosts can contain hundreds of Long-eared Owls.

Flocking in birds happens when the benefits of company – like extra eyes to find food and spot danger, the added safety of hiding in a crowd, or more chances to meet a mate – outweigh the downsides, such as competition for food or attracting attention from predators. Some birds, including Long-eared Owls, are solitary by day but roost in groups, sharing body heat. They might also watch the flight paths other birds take when they leave the roosts, as this can help give ideas for good places to look for food. However, they don't want company when actually hunting, and might fight if they meet at this time.

look for dense cover – or press themselves against a
tree trunk, relying on their stillness and camouflaged
feathers to stay out of sight.

Owls don't stay busy all night. If they catch a
large enough meal early on, they may spend the rest
of the night resting or attending to other tasks. These
might include scouting for future nest sites, preening
their feathers, or singing to defend their territory or
attract a mate. Some species are especially vocal.
Male Eurasian Scops Owls, for example, sing on

and off all through the night when they first claim a territory, sometimes for over an hour at a time.

During the early part of the breeding season, the female owl stays in or near the nest. She incubates the eggs and broods the young chicks day and night, taking only brief breaks. Meanwhile, the male must hunt for himself, his mate and their growing family. As the chicks get bigger, both parents spend most of their waking time hunting to keep everyone fed.

Breeding

Winter is a lean time in nature, and for the five owl species that breed in the British Isles, the start of the year is all about survival. By late winter, though, many owls are already bonding with mates and preparing for the season ahead, and as spring approaches, more signs of courtship begin to appear.

Tawny Owls are among the earliest to nest. Established pairs often lay their eggs in mid-March, usually in the same tree cavity they used the year before. Short-eared Owls, on the other hand, take a more relaxed approach. They may not settle on a nesting site until well into spring, and often don't lay eggs until mid-May. Short-eared Owl chicks grow up fast, though, so earlier nesters occasionally have a second brood in the same year.

Nesting – the numbers

Breeding takes up three or more months of an owl's year – from incubating eggs to raising chicks until they leave the nest, and then looking after them for at least a few more weeks as they learn to hunt for themselves.

Here's a snapshot of the typical nesting timeline for the five owl species in the British Isles:

Species	First egg laid	Incubation	Fledging	Clutch size (range)
Barn Owl	~6 May	32 days	56 days	5 (2–12)
Tawny Owl	~23 March	30 days	36 days	3 (1–6)
Little Owl	~23 April	30 days	37 days	3 (2–6)
Long-eared Owl	~12 April	28 days	31 days	4 (2–6)
Short-eared Owl	Highly variable	26 days	28 days	5 (2–9)

(Data from the BTO)

Owls don't build nests in the traditional sense. Most prefer to find a ready-made cavity – a hole in a tree, a crevice in a crag, or even an old nest left behind by another bird.

Smaller owls often use abandoned woodpecker holes. For example, Northern Pygmy Owls in northern Europe favour old Great Spotted Woodpecker nests, while the slightly larger Tengmalm's Owl prefers those made by Black Woodpeckers. A small entrance helps keep predators out –

WHOSE NEST IS IT ANYWAY?

....

Competition for good nest sites can be fierce. The problem isn't necessarily other owls of the same species – territorial defence by singing usually keeps them at bay. But many other birds nest in holes too, and a prime spot can be worth fighting for.

A Barn Owl might have to defend its nest from Little Owls, Kestrels, Jackdaws, Stock Doves and even Ring-necked Parakeets. Nest box cameras have revealed just how intense these battles can be.

Tawny Owls are big and tough enough to defend their nests against most would-be invaders, but even they can be vulnerable while incubating. In some cases, Jackdaws have filled open-topped nesting hollows with sticks, trapping and killing the female owl incubating her eggs inside.

especially agile hunters like martens, which could threaten both the mother owl and her chicks.

Larger owls often nest in tree hollows, formed when a branch breaks or the crown of a tree snaps off and the surrounding wood begins to decay. They may also reuse the old nests of other birds. Long-eared Owls often settle into abandoned crow or Common Buzzard nests, while Short-eared Owls sometimes nest directly on the ground, hidden among grasses and low vegetation.

Owl eggs are white and very round. The female begins incubating as soon as she lays her first egg, so the chicks hatch in sequence rather than all at once. This gives the first-hatched chick a head start – it's bigger, stronger and more likely to win any battle for food than its siblings.

In lean years, it's better for the parents to raise one healthy chick than several undernourished ones. But in good years, the whole brood may survive to fledging age, and owls can adjust their clutch size depending on food availability.

When the chicks are small, the mother stays with them to keep them warm and safe. She feeds them tiny bites of prey brought by the male. Soon, they're able to swallow small prey whole, and both parents leave the nest to hunt.

Over time, the nest cavity becomes messy – full of droppings, pellets and leftover prey – attracting flies. In North America, screech owls have a clever

FLUFF AND FEATHERS

Baby owls are blind and helpless, covered in a sparse layer of down. At this stage, they need constant care from their mother, who keeps them warm and defends them from danger. As the larger of the sexes, she's well equipped for the job.

As the chicks grow, the first down is replaced with a thicker, warmer coat called mesoptile plumage – it's still very soft but is more recognisably feather-like. Around this time, many chicks also develop a distinct facial disc, giving them a more owl-like appearance (though their markings often differ from the adult's).

Eventually, the mesoptile plumage is replaced by juvenile feathers – the first set of fully functional, insulating and flight-ready plumage that will carry them into independent life.

solution: they release live blind snakes into the nest. These tiny insect-eating snakes act as natural pest controllers.

Once the chicks fledge, they gradually become more independent. Some species wander away from the nest well before they can fly, watching insects and small animals with growing interest. Their first catch is often an insect that strays too close.

Learning to hunt takes time, and parents continue to bring food for several weeks after fledging. This is a crucial period for the young owls to build strength and gain weight – a buffer against the challenges of independence.

When they leave their parents' territory, the young owls must fend for themselves and avoid conflict with adult owls whose territories they might accidentally enter. They're also more vulnerable to predators than adults. Even the young of large species, like Eurasian Eagle-owls, must watch out for lynxes, wolves and other dangers, choosing safe roosts and being cautious when hunting on the ground.

Conflict

If you've ever watched a pair of Little Owls, you'll know how affectionate they can be – sitting close together, gently preening each other's heads and necks. In the Americas, their cousin the Burrowing

Owl takes sociability even further, living in loose colonies and defending shared nesting areas as a group. But these are exceptions. Most owls are solitary by nature, and even long-term mates approach each other with caution.

MOBBING

Owls don't just face rivals and predators –
they also attract unwanted attention from
smaller birds. These birds might be potential
prey under different circumstances, but when
they spot a sleeping owl, they often band
together to drive it away.

Many birdwatchers have found a hidden
Tawny Owl by watching the behaviour of
songbirds – diving, calling, and eventually
forcing the owl to move on.

Young, territory-less Tawnies are especially
vulnerable to this kind of harassment. Being
mobbed can make it harder for them to rest
or hunt, increasing
the risk of starvation,
which, from the
mobbers' point of
view, is a win.
Even larger
birds like crows may
chase and harry a flying or
roosting owl. Mobbing is risky
for the attackers, but the reward is
peace of mind – a safer night's sleep
with the nocturnal threat gone.

In species that hold territories year-round, the fiercest battles happen in winter. Young owls born the previous summer are still searching for a territory of their own, and may challenge established adults.

These contests often begin with vocal duels, followed by dramatic displays – wings spread wide, feathers fluffed, bodies puffed up to look as intimidating as possible.

Physical fights are rare, but when they happen, they can be ferocious. Even species like Short-eared Owls, which aren't territorial in winter, may clash over feeding grounds, showing talons or grappling in mid-air if another owl gets too close.

Travel

. . . .

For sedentary species like the Tawny Owl, the first year of life is often the only time that they travel a significant distance. Their strategy is simple: settle down or die trying.

For more nomadic species, wandering is a way of life. Both Short-eared and Long-eared Owls regularly cross the North Sea – and other oceans – when they leave their breeding areas in autumn. A Short-eared Owl might even nest in two or more different places over a single summer, travelling many kilometres between attempts.

In the Arctic, species like the Snowy Owl and Northern Hawk Owl head south in harsh weather. The Eurasian Scops Owl of southern Europe is a true migrant, spending its winters in sub-Saharan Africa. Like other migratory birds, owls sometimes turn up in unexpected places, and they have even been known to hitch a ride on boats.

ADVENTURERS

....

Owls vary greatly in how far they travel, but there are always outliers. The table below shows some remarkable journeys recorded by the British Trust for Ornithology (BTO), based on ringing data from owls either tagged or recovered in the British Isles.

Species	Distance travelled	From/to
Barn Owl	1,105km	Essex to Girona, Spain
Tawny Owl	688km	Scottish Highlands to Carmarthenshire
Little Owl	182km	Dorset to Herefordshire
Long-eared Owl	3,280km	Cumbria to Mariy El, Russia
Short-eared Owl	2,537km	Lincoln to Vologda Oblast, Russia

(Data from the British Trust for Ornithology)

Like all other animals, owls have to live in (or travel to) places where they can find food. What they eat, though, and how they catch it, is surprisingly varied, and that's what we explore in the next chapter.

CHAPTER FOUR

What's on the Menu?

You have probably seen photos
of owls with their prey – a Tawny or
Long-eared Owl clutching a lifeless mouse
in its bill, ready to swallow it head-first.
It's a moment that tells a bigger story: the
mouse probably had no warning, no chance to
escape. Silently, swiftly, the owl struck – aided
by an array of anatomical and behavioural
adaptations honed for stealth and precision.
Hours later, the bones of that mouse will
reappear, almost intact, bound together
in a compact pellet, regurgitated and
left behind like a signature.

Across the world, owls share many traits in how they hunt and feed. However, their diets are far from uniform. Some species specialise, relying almost exclusively on a single type of prey. Others are opportunists, taking whatever they can find – from insects, fish and amphibians to birds and mammals. This diversity reflects not only their habitats, but also their evolutionary flexibility: owls are predators, but no two species hunt in quite the same way.

More than mice

All five owls that are widespread across the British Isles will eat mice. But none of them are true mouse-hunting specialists. Broaden that out to *small rodents*, however, and you account for the core diets of four out of five species. One rodent dominates: the Field Vole (also known as the Short-tailed Vole). With an estimated population of almost 60 million, this plump little package of protein is the most abundant mammal in Great Britain, and a vital food source for many birds of prey.

The Short-eared Owl is especially dependent on Field Voles, which can make up a large percentage of its diet. This owl's regular nomadic movements are closely tied to vole population cycles, and its own numbers rise and fall in step with those of its favourite prey.

What's on the Menu?

TONIGHT'S MENU

Here's a taste of what's on the menu
for the five resident owls in
the British Isles:

Tawny Owl

Appetiser
Bird of the day, from a choice of
100 species (but most likely a sparrow)
Main
Tasting platter of rodents and shrews
Dessert
Fish, worm and frog surprise,
garnished with carrion

Barn Owl

Appetiser
Wood Mouse
Main
Field Vole
Dessert
Common Shrew

Little Owl

Appetiser
Selection of beetles

Main
Field Vole

Dessert
Selection of moths, earthworms and more beetles

Long-eared Owl

Appetiser
Field Vole

Main
Medley of small birds

Dessert
Bank Vole

Short-eared Owl

Appetiser
Field Vole

Main
Field Vole

Dessert
Field Vole

The Tawny Owl, by contrast, has a much broader diet. As a strongly territorial and sedentary species, it must meet all its nutritional needs within its own $0.12–0.2$ km^2 patch, and that means being flexible. An ideal Tawny territory in the British Isles will

support plenty of Wood Mice, Bank Voles, shrews and other small mammals, which are its preferred prey. But when these are scarce, the Tawny turns to small and medium-sized birds (more than 100 species have been recorded as prey in Europe), bats, amphibians, fish (which it can catch live from ponds), earthworms, large insects such as moths and beetles, and even carrion, including roadkill and leftovers from other predators.

Little Owls, also sedentary by nature, are similarly adaptable. Being smaller, they rely more heavily on invertebrates, especially beetles and earthworms.

Further afield, some owl diets become more specialised. Some species, like the enormous Blakiston's Fish Owl of eastern Asia, hunt fish almost exclusively. Eurasian Eagle-owls are skilled and strong enough to tackle Hedgehogs, unravelling and disembowelling them. Tiny scops owls and the even smaller Flammulated Owl (opposite) of the Americas feed mainly on moths, which they catch in flight or pick from tree foliage. The equally small but more aggressive saw-whet owls regularly kill other birds, even some that are larger than themselves.

Even within a single species, diets can vary dramatically. On remote islands, some populations of Short-eared Owls never encounter voles at all. Instead, they hunt storm-petrels at dusk, lying in wait for them as the seabirds return to their burrows after a day at sea.

Hunting tactics

. . . .

Most owls rely on a method known as 'sit-and-wait hunting'. The principle is simple: if your prey is capable of running away, sometimes the best strategy is to stay still and quiet and let it come to you – the result can be a very low-effort meal. For a Tawny Owl, this means returning to favourite perches within its territory, places it knows have a good view and a clear flight path to the ground. From here, it watches and listens for movement below. One silent, speedy swoop later, and the owl has its meal.

A Tawny typically needs to eat four to six small rodents per night – around 75g of food, or roughly 10 per cent of its body weight. In good conditions, this is easily achieved. In poor conditions, it can be a real challenge.

The other main hunting method is actively searching in flight. Barn Owls, Long-eared Owls and Short-eared Owls favour this approach, and Tawnies will sometimes adopt it too. The owl flies low over the ground, allowing it to scan and listen for movement below. Its exceptional hearing and silent flight make this tactic highly effective. The bird may hover briefly to pinpoint its prey before making the final pounce.

This method can yield quicker results than sit-and-wait, but it is more weather-dependent. A light

breeze provides helpful, energy-saving uplift, but strong winds or heavy rain make controlled flight difficult and interfere with the owl's ability to hear its prey. In such conditions, reverting to sit-and-wait may be more productive. Prolonged bad weather can force owls to take more desperate measures – hunting in daylight or switching to less suitable prey.

MUG OR BE MUGGED

....

A winter meadow in the late afternoon can be a wonderful place to watch birds of prey in the British Isles. If there are lots of voles in that area, you might see Short-eared and Barn Owls sharing hunting grounds with Hen Harriers and Kestrels. All of them are after the same prey, but not all of them catch it themselves. There's another option: steal your meal from another hunter.

The technique is simple in theory – grab a vole with your talons. The twist is that the vole is already firmly in someone else's grip. To succeed, the thief must approach with agility, strike with precision, and cling on with tenacity, hoping that the original hunter gives up the struggle.

This behaviour, known as kleptoparasitism, may be attempted by any of these four birds of prey. But the most frequent offender is the Kestrel, and the most frequent victim of its felonious foraging is the Barn Owl. As both species are widespread year-round, these aerial thefts can be witnessed in all seasons. During the breeding season, repeated losses to Kestrels can significantly increase the workload for parent Barn Owls – a strong incentive to hunt at night, when Kestrels are less active.

For birdwatchers, this can be a gift. A calm early evening following a stormy night is often a great time to look for actively hunting owls, especially Barn Owls. Stand with the breeze behind you and you may find an owl flying towards you, making use of the uplift.

Owls strike with their feet first, using a powerful grip and sharp, curved talons to pierce and hold their prey. This may be enough to kill it outright, but if not, the owl delivers a finishing blow with its bill once the prey is securely pinned. It may eat the prey on the spot or carry it to a safer perch using its feet, or its bill if the prey is small.

If you see an owl flying a long distance with prey, it's probably heading back to its nest to feed chicks or its mate.

Other hunting methods include flying close to hedgerows to flush out roosting birds, snatching young birds from nests (sometimes by forcing access through dense cover), or even chasing prey on foot. Little Owls, with their long legs and surprising speed, are particularly fond of this method.

Tawny Owls have also been observed catching fish and frogs, either by snatching them from the water in flight, or by wading into the shallows and grabbing them.

With their incredible hearing, owls can catch prey that they can't see at all. Northern species like the Great Grey Owl can hear a vole moving under snow cover, and swoop down and punch their talons through the snow in exactly the right spot.

Eating

. . . .

Swallowing a mouse whole is no small feat – so why don't owls break their food down into more manageable pieces first? The answer lies in efficiency. Although swallowing whole prey is physically more demanding, it's also quicker. The faster an owl consumes its catch, the less chance there is of losing it to a rival or scavenger.

Some prey, however, is simply too large to go down in one go. In those cases, owls will tear it into chunks first. Though even then, the pieces they swallow are still substantial.

Whole prey ingestion means owls consume a lot of material that offers them little or no nutritional value. This includes bones, feathers, fur, fish scales, insect wings and legs, and other tough or indigestible prey parts. These are dealt with in a specialised part of their digestive system: the gizzard. This muscular organ compacts the waste into a smoothish pellet, which is then regurgitated through the mouth. The rest of the meal continues through the gut, where nutrients are absorbed and the remaining waste is excreted as liquid droppings, along with uric acid filtered from the blood by the kidneys.

Owls have a simple gut compared to some other birds, because what's left of their meals after pellet production is very nutrient-dense and easy to digest.

STUDYING PELLETS

. . . .

Owls are a gift to biologists, thanks to their habit of producing pellets. While many birds regurgitate pellets, owl pellets are especially useful: they're compact, stable, and packed with large, intact prey remains that are usually easy to identify.

Owls tend to drop pellets at just a few favourite roosts or at their nests, leading to large accumulations. If you examine a pellet from a medium-sized or large owl species, you can often see whole skulls and other bones, revealing what the owl has eaten. This not only reveals the owl's diet but can also confirm the presence of prey species that are otherwise hard to detect, offering valuable insights into the wider ecosystem.

We humans have only been studying owl behaviour and biology in depth for a few decades, and our studies bring new surprises every year. However, we have noticed owls, watched them, created artworks of them and told stories about them for far longer. In the next chapter, we explore this shared history.

CHAPTER FIVE

Owls
and Us

When did you last see an owl in
the wild? For many people, the answer
is 'a long time ago' – or perhaps 'never'.
And yet, if asked to draw one, most of us
could sketch a recognisable owl with ease:
round face, forward-facing eyes, hooked
beak, a pair of feathered tufts on its head.
We know what owls look like, even
if we've never met one.

This is the paradox of the owl. These birds are elusive in life, yet ever-present in our imagination. They appear in myths and stories, on book covers and bank logos, in cartoons, coats of arms and conservation campaigns. They are symbols of wisdom, omens of death, guardians of the night – their meanings as varied as the cultures that revere or fear them.

Owls are among the most recognisable birds on the planet, not because we see them often, but because we see them *everywhere* – in language, in art, in logos, and in the stories we tell about the natural world.

From Athena to Arthur

. . . .

The ancient Greek goddess of wisdom, Athena, has an owl companion in many of her depictions, as does her Roman counterpart Minerva. The link is retained in the scientific name *Athene*, denoting the genus to which the Little Owl and its close relatives belong. Athena's owl may indeed have been a Little Owl – the species is widespread in Greece and the Mediterranean in general. Merlin the wizard, another figure associated with ineffable wisdom, also had an owl familiar, Archimedes, in *The Sword in the Stone* (1938), T. H. White's novel based on the Arthurian legends. The link between owls and wisdom may be inspired by our admiration of their ability to see in the dark – indeed, wisdom itself might be defined as the ability to see truths others cannot.

Another very well-known literary owl is part of the menagerie that populates the woodlands in A. A. Milne's *Winnie-the-Pooh* stories (1926). This Owl, however, is more self-important than wise and is there to remind us that those who affect superiority by using big words don't necessarily know the meaning of what they are saying. Milne's owl (a Tawny, going by E. H. Shepard's beautiful illustrations) is one of many owls that have been fully fleshed characters in their own right in assorted stories of print and screen.

FIVE FAMOUS
FICTIONAL OWLS

....

Hedwig – Harry Potter's companion from the moment Harry enters the wizarding world, Hedwig the Snowy Owl is one of J. K. Rowling's most beloved creations. Like all owls in the wizarding world, she was a messenger, but was also a fierce and loyal friend. Her death in *Harry Potter and the Deathly Hallows* (2007) marked Harry's transition to adulthood as well as the beginning of a final, all-changing battle between good and evil.

The Owl (and the Pussycat) – Edward Lear wrote and published numerous 'nonsense poems' in the late nineteenth century, and this poem, published in 1871, is one of the best known. The owl of the poem went to sea with his feline lady-love, and married her in an exotic land. Lear's illustration for the poem shows what appears to be a Long-eared Owl, playing the guitar and singing for the cat as they float along in a beautiful pea-green boat. He holds and plays the instrument rather awkwardly with his feet – Lear avoiding the modern trick of drawing a bird's flight feathers as fingers when depicting them handling an object.

Big Mama – The 1981 Disney animated film *The Fox and The Hound* was an unusually gritty example of the genre, documenting the friendship and subsequent catastrophic falling-out between orphaned Red Fox cub Tod and hunting dog puppy Copper. Big Mama, a Great Horned Owl, was one of several forest birds who watched over and guided Tod, the young fox, in his early months. She was wise, as befits any fictional owl, but also a gentle and nurturing grandmotherly figure who helps raise Tod.

Plop – The children's picture book *The Owl Who Was Afraid of the Dark*, written by Jill Tomlinson, was published in 1968 and has stayed in print ever since. Baby Barn Owl Plop overcomes his fear of darkness after speaking with assorted people and animals who show him the beauty and magic of night-time. Clinicians have recommended this beautifully illustrated (by Joanne Cole in the original edition and Paul Howard in the modern edition) book to help both adults and children deal with a phobia of darkness and night.

The Owl (and the Nightingale) –
This Middle English poem, written in the
twelfth or thirteenth century by a person
or persons unknown and since interpreted
and reimagined by various authors, takes the
form of an overheard verbal contest between
the two female birds, who are bitter rivals in
every way. They viciously mock each other's
appearance, voice, morals and value to society,
and conclude their discussion by flying off to
ask a local personage, Nicholas of Guildford,
to decide which of them is superior. Despite
much scholarly attention, any deeper
meaning to the work remains elusive, but in
its snappiness and ferocity, it would stand
up alongside any modern battle of words.

In the British Isles, owls in stories both ancient and modern are often cast as harbingers of doom. Shakespeare's portentous owls included the one whose cry marked Macbeth's murder of King Duncan – 'It was the owl that shrieked, the fatal bellman', as Lady Macbeth put it. In *King Henry VI, Part 3*, the king insulted Richard III with: 'The owl shrieked at thy birth, an evil sign.' The owl that shrieks most noticeably is the Barn Owl, suggesting this was the species most familiar to Shakespeare and his peers, out of the four available in the British Isles at the time (this was before the Little Owl was introduced). This makes sense, as Barn Owls, then as now, often nested in old buildings and did a fine job controlling mice and rats around farmyards. However, some owl illustrations of Shakespeare's time show an owl with ear tufts instead, for example an apparent Long-eared Owl eyeing the reader thoughtfully while writing in a book of its own, on the front page of *The Owles Almanacke* (see illustration on page 89), a 1618 collection of curious tales and anecdotes.

Folklore and legend

Folk stories about animals abound in all cultures. Many carry a moral lesson, while others offer imaginative explanations for how certain animals acquired their most striking traits.

One story from the indigenous peoples of Quebec tells of the Northern Saw-whet Owl – a fierce but very tiny species – which was once the largest of all owls. It had a booming voice that it used once too often, irritating the Great Spirit, who punished it by shrinking both its body and its voice, the latter from a boom to a squeak.

In an Inuit tale, the first owl was originally a human girl, transformed by witchcraft into a long-billed bird. In her panic, she flew face-first into the side of a house, squashing her straight bill into a hook – a detail that echoes the curved beak of many owl species today.

Owl calls carry different meanings across cultures. Among some communities in India, the screeches of an owl function similarly to the Magpie-counting rhyme of England – 'one for sorrow, two for joy' – with each owl cry carrying a different omen. One screech may foretell a death, two a triumph, and so on, up to eight (another death, but an unexpected one) and nine (good luck for

the listener). Anyone who hears eight cries is caught between hope and despair, waiting for just one more screech.

In England, Wales and some other parts of Europe, the hoot of a Tawny Owl may be taken to announce a death, a birth or – in some older folk traditions – that a young woman nearby has just lost her virginity.

Egypt's owls

The ancient Egyptians knew – and in many cases revered – their birds. More than 70 identifiable species appear in Egyptian art, including the Barn Owl and aptly named Pharaoh Eagle-owl. Fanciful hybrids of these two species were also depicted.

Although the ancient Egyptian pantheon may have lacked a specific owl deity (the best-known avian god, Horus, has the head of a Lanner Falcon), owls were nonetheless respected and venerated.

The owl hieroglyph, typically shown side-on with the face turned forwards to look at the reader, represents the letter *m* when used within words. It also appears as a standalone symbol for various short words.

Owls feature in Egyptian wall paintings too. A scene from the tomb of Neferhotep shows a Barn Owl nesting among ducks and other wildfowl, its wings spread protectively as a mongoose slinks towards its chicks.

Some real owls, of several species, were also mummified and placed in catacombs. These were votive offerings, left at sacred sites for religious purposes, with no intention that they be moved. In total, millions of mummified birds and animals have been found across Egypt.

One of the world's most recently described owl species, the Desert Tawny Owl, is native to Egypt. A bird of rocky, rugged desert terrain, it was formally identified in 2015 – though it may well have been known to the keen-eyed naturalists of ancient Egypt thousands of years ago.

Places and names

In England, several place names hint at the historical presence – or cultural significance – of owls. Some are obvious, such as the Owlerton district of Sheffield, which lends its name and emblem to the football club Sheffield Wednesday, known as *The Owls*.

Others are more subtle, containing the Old English word for owl – *ule* – such as Ullenwood in Gloucestershire, and Ulcombe in Kent. Both 'owl' and *ule* echo the sound of an owl's hoot, and share linguistic roots with the evocative word 'ululate', meaning to howl or wail. Rhostyllen, a village in Gwynedd, may reference the Welsh word *tylluan*, meaning 'owl'.

There are also numerous Owl Roads, Owl Streets, and a fair scattering of woods and copses named for owls, often reflecting either the presence of the birds or their symbolic resonance.

Readers who were members of the Brownies, a social and educational organisation for girls aged seven to ten, may remember their own 'Brown Owl', the title given to the adult leader of a Brownies group. One of the defining features of the Brownies is that girls complete activities and earn badges, which they wear on their uniforms. Group leaders also wear a Brown Owl badge, and their assistant helpers may adopt owl-themed names such as Barn Owl, Snowy Owl or Tawny Owl. Not all leaders choose owl names, but they remain popular for their reassuring connotations of wisdom and guidance.

The actual bird referred to by 'Brown Owl' is the Tawny Owl, and brown owl is probably the most widely used alternative name for this species, though it is rarely heard today.

The Barn Owl, meanwhile, has accumulated a remarkable number of nicknames over the centuries, many of them inspired by its eerie voice. These include screech owl, white owl, Billy Whit, church owl, yellow owl, rat owl, roarer, pudge, Jenny Howlett and at least a dozen others. In North America, the American Barn Owl has also been known as the demon owl and death owl, names that reflect its ghostly appearance and haunting call.

Owls in art

Owls have long been popular subjects in art, with countless artists across history painting, sculpting and sketching them in their own distinctive styles.

Pablo Picasso was particularly fond of owls, producing numerous owl-themed works in sketch, paint and ceramics. His vase-shaped owl ceramics are especially charming – some even function as jugs, with the bird's bill serving as the spout.

Picasso

In 2024, one of his ceramics sold at auction in London for £2.46 million.

John James Audubon, author and artist of _Birds of America_ (published between 1827 and 1838 and now considered one of the most valuable books in the world), included several North American owl species in his collection. Renowned for his precision and attention to detail – unmatched in his lifetime – Audubon also imbued his birds with drama and expressiveness. His painting of male and female Snowy Owls, glowing against a storm-darkened sky, is especially striking. Equally memorable is his portrayal of two American Barn Owls, wings spread, one clutching a luckless chipmunk.

While many individual prints were sold separately, a complete bound copy of *Birds of America* fetched a staggering £7.3 million at auction in London in 2010.

Contemporary artists have also embraced the owl. Tracy Emin and Lucian Freud have both produced owl-themed works, as have many specialist wildlife and bird artists such as David Shepherd and Robert Bateman.

Owls have also appeared in the work of cartoonists, notably Gary Larson, creator of the enduringly popular *Far Side* comic. In one strip, two owls sit with their backs to the viewer. One sneaks its wing around the other to perform the classic 'who tapped my shoulder?' prank. The final panel shows the pranked owl spinning its head 180 degrees to catch the culprit – a perfect blend of avian anatomy and human humour.

Owls in science

With their elusive ways, owls present ornithologists with some significant challenges, and they have inspired some ingenious solutions.

Bird ringing, the practice of ornithologists marking birds with a uniquely numbered ring fitted around their lower leg, has been used for more than a century to study migration, site loyalty, longevity and other aspects of avian life history. Owls, however, are harder to catch than many species: they are nocturnal and acutely sensitive to disturbance.

Nest boxes have helped overcome this problem. Scientists can open the box to ring chicks easily, and parents can be caught using a mist net placed at the entrance of the box.

Ringing studies often suffer high 'wastage' – most ringed birds are never seen again. Those that are recovered, dead or alive, usually provide just one extra data point: *date found* to pair with *date ringed*. What happens in between remains a mystery.

To fill these gaps, researchers now use geolocators and GPS trackers, mounted on tiny backpack-style harnesses designed to fall off after a set time. Making trackers light enough for owls has taken years, but GPS units now weigh only a couple of grams and

can be carried by birds as light as 70g. Geolocators, which record light levels to infer position, are even smaller – some models weigh less than one-third of a gram – but they must be retrieved to download data.

Tracking reveals extraordinary details: exact flight paths, stopovers and timing. The BTO's work with Short-eared Owls has shown how these nomadic owls travel. One female, for example, nested in Scotland in spring 2018, then crossed the North Sea to Norway a few months later, where she nested again.

The study of bird sound has advanced dramatically since the early 2000s, thanks to sophisticated recording equipment and computerised waveform analysis. Pioneered by the UK-based Sound Approach team, this work has mapped the ranges of rare owls worldwide and uncovered the complex vocal habits of familiar species.

Owls also contribute to science through their pellets, which provide a snapshot of prey species in their habitat – a simple but powerful tool for ecological research.

The reality of owls, it turns out, is no less weird and wonderful than their representations in lore and legend. In the next chapter, we look at how humanity in general – and we as individuals – can help to ensure that the owls of the future thrive and survive on an increasingly pressured planet.

MODERN SYMBOLISM
— THE LOGO

....

With its easily recognisable shape and associations with wisdom – and by extension, with good judgement – the owl appears in logos for companies of all kinds. A standard depiction of an owl, however simple, has the bird making direct eye contact with us – this creates an image that says 'I am trustworthy' just as much as 'I am wise'.

One of the most familiar is Duo, the green owl mascot of *Duolingo*, the language-learning app. Duo (full name Duo Keyshauna Renee

Lingo) is designed to be friendly, encouraging and slightly mischievous – a visual embodiment of the app's gamified approach to learning. In England, the football team Sheffield Wednesday is represented by a white owl above the motto *Consilio et Animis* ('By wisdom and courage'). The team itself is nicknamed *The Owls*, after the Owlerton region of Sheffield, as we saw on page 94 in the section on owl-related place names.

The American internet company Tripadvisor, known for its user-generated reviews of hotels, restaurants and tourist attractions, uses a stylised owl's head in green and black as its logo – a nod to the idea of seeing clearly and making informed choices.

More playfully – and controversially – Hooters, the American restaurant chain, uses an owl logo with exaggerated oversized eyes that resemble a particular mammalian rather than avian body part. The name itself is a double entendre, and the owl serves as both mascot and pun. Perhaps surprisingly for birds that spend so much time doing very little, owls are also used in the emblems of a number of American athletics programs.

CHAPTER SIX

Protecting Owls and Their Future

As we saw in chapter 2, owls have a long evolutionary history – species have emerged, flourished and disappeared over millions of years. Today, with more than 200 living species, owls remain one of the more diverse and successful orders of birds. Yet many are now under threat. Habitat loss, climate change, pollution and human disturbance are placing growing pressure on owl populations around the world.

Despite their elusive nature, owls enjoy a high public profile and a largely positive image. This has helped drive support for their conservation – from nest box schemes and habitat restoration to research and education. But in a world increasingly shaped by human activity, conservationists face difficult decisions. Resources are limited and the needs of vulnerable species are many.

The good news is that we are not powerless. Whether through supporting conservation efforts, protecting habitats, or simply learning more and sharing what we know, each of us can play a part in securing a future for owls – and for the wider ecosystems they depend on.

Survival and lifespan

. . . .

As with most wild birds, any individual owl is far more likely to die young than to reach old age. Within a brood, the first-hatched chick has the best chance of survival; in lean times, the smallest and youngest usually perish first. If a predator discovers the nest, there are likely to be no survivors. Likewise, if one parent dies during incubation or while the chicks are still small, the outcome is almost certainly fatal for the brood.

After fledging, inexperience makes young owls highly vulnerable to misadventure, predation and starvation – risks that only intensify during their first winter.

If an owl survives its first year, its prospects improve dramatically. By then, it has mastered the basic skills of survival and stands a good chance of living for several more years. Owls in captivity often live for a decade or two, sometimes longer, before succumbing to age-related conditions. In the wild, however, few reach old age; most die from starvation, accidents or predation, and even the slightest age-related weakness would make any of these more likely to happen.

Many accidental deaths involve human-made hazards. Barn Owls, for example, are particularly vulnerable to collisions with vehicles, drowning in

HOW LONG DO OWLS LIVE?

....

Decades of ringing recovery data give us a good idea of how long different owl species typically live if they survive their first year. Among these records are truly remarkable outliers that lived far longer than average, showing how rare a natural old age is in wild birds.

Species	Typical adult lifespan	Oldest known (UK)	Oldest known (Europe)
Barn Owl	~4 years	15 years 7 months	30 years 9 months (Netherlands)
Tawny Owl	~4 years	23 years 5 months	23 years 5 months (UK)
Little Owl	~3 years	13 years 10 months	15 years 4 months (Germany)
Long-eared Owl	~4 years	12 years 10 months	21 years 10 months (Netherlands)
Short-eared Owl	Insufficient data	6 years 7 months	20 years 9 months (Germany)

(Data from the BTO and EURING)

livestock drinking troughs, or becoming tangled up in litter such as balloon strings. They may also get trapped inside buildings while seeking nest sites.

Threats

When a population of wild animals is known to be declining – over a long enough period to rule out natural fluctuations – identifying the factors driving that decline can be straightforward or complex. In most cases, human activity plays a role.

One clear-cut example occurred in the British Isles in the 1950s, soon after the advent of the widespread use of a new class of insecticides. DDT and other organochlorides proved highly effective against crop-eating insects, but they also accumulated in the food chain, poisoning other wildlife, including predators. Birds of prey died in large numbers and also suffered sublethal effects that reduced their breeding success, including plummeting fertility and eggs with thin, fragile shells. By the time these impacts were understood and the chemicals banned, populations of farmland birds of prey like Barn Owls had crashed.

Today, owls face a new threat: rodenticide poisoning. Rat poisons like brodifacoum are widely used on farms and around pheasant-rearing pens on shooting estates.

A TALE OF TWO OWLS

....

In North America, two closely related owl
species have come into conflict because of
human-caused habitat change. Extensive
deforestation has allowed the Barred Owl,
which prefers less forested habitat, to
spread westwards into the natural range
of the Spotted Owl. Where the two species
meet, the Barred Owl competes with and
displaces the Spotted, creating a complex
conservation problem. One proposed solution
– a controversial cull of Barred Owls – has
been widely debated but lacks long-term
sustainability.

The biggest global problem affecting wildlife is habitat loss, as humans convert natural landscapes to other uses, or alter land management in ways that deplete its ecological value. In the British Isles during the twentieth century, sweeping changes to farming practices aimed at boosting productivity included widespread removal of hedgerows, alteration of river courses, draining of marshlands, and the use of machinery and herbicides that reduced native wild plants on farmland. These changes made large tracts of countryside less hospitable to insects and small mammals, with inevitable knock-on effects on owl populations. Deforestation, removal of nesting trees, and replacing mature woodland with non-native conifer plantations also directly remove owl habitat.

PERSECUTION

··············

As if owls didn't have enough to contend with, many species have been deliberately hunted and killed in large numbers over the last few centuries, and some still are.

In some cultures, owls are hunted for meat, as part of the widespread consumption of 'bushmeat' (wild birds and mammals of all kinds). Other owls are targeted because they compete with human interests: for example, Tawny Owls were killed on sight by gamekeepers in the nineteenth and twentieth centuries in Great Britain because they occasionally preyed on young pheasants. They now have full legal protection, but are still occasionally killed by illegal traps or poisons (often placed to target other predatory species).

Superstition-driven killing is another factor, and remains common in some regions – for instance, in Jamaica, where traditional fears about the native Jamaican Owl (opposite) persist despite the birds having legal protection.

Interestingly, superstition can sometimes be protective rather than deadly. In Madagascar, traditional religious taboos (*fady*) identify owls as carriers of evil spirits but prohibit harming them, lest the spirits be angered.

Wildlife can adapt to habitat changes over time, through the process of evolution, but today many of the changes are happening much too quickly.

The impact of climate change – and related shifts in weather patterns – on wildlife is increasingly evident in the twenty-first century. Some observed impacts on owls include a northward spread of species such as the Burrowing Owl of North America, and a decline in Snowy Owls in the High Arctic. Adaptations are also emerging: in Finland, brown-morph Tawny Owls are becoming more numerous, while the paler grey morphs are declining, reflecting milder, less snowy winters.

Introduced non-native species can also pose problems for wildlife. In the British Isles, the arrival of the North American Grey Squirrel famously devastated native Red Squirrel populations. Of the five owls found in the British Isles, one – the Little Owl – is itself non-native, deliberately introduced from mainland Europe in the nineteenth century. As a hole-nesting species, it competes for nest sites with native species and other introduced species, such as the Ring-necked Parakeet and Mandarin Duck. Its overall impact has been minimal, but as a non-native species, the Little Owl is not a conservation priority.

Protecting, supporting, thriving

. . . .

Today in the British Isles, all owls – like other wild birds – enjoy full legal protection. It is illegal to harm them or destroy their active nests. Retaining and enforcing these laws is the essential first step in protecting our owls. Barn Owls have an extra layer of legal protection: in both the UK and Ireland, they may not be disturbed at or near their active nests. If the Snowy Owl ever breeds in the British Isles again, it will receive similar safeguards.

Watching over our owls

. . . .

The British Trust for Ornithology (BTO) monitors the UK's wild birds through nationwide surveys, including regular breeding pair counts and year-round observations on predefined 1-km squares. Decades of data reveal how owls' populations and ranges have changed, and the picture is mixed. Of the five species, four show declines or shrinking ranges. Two are now classed as Amber on the UK's Species of Conservation Concern list, meaning they need extra study and more support to help their populations to stabilise and recover.

Species	UK population	Recent trend	Distribution change	Status
Barn Owl	4,000 pairs	+231% 1995–2023	+3.6%	Green
Tawny Owl	50,000 pairs	-43% 1995–2023	-25.1%	Amber
Little Owl	3,600 pairs	-79.2% 1995–2023	-53.4%	None*
Long-eared Owl	1,800 pairs	Not known	Not known	Green
Short-eared Owl	620 pairs	Not known	Not known	Amber

*Little Owl is non-native and not a conservation priority
(Data from the BTO)

Meeting owls' habitat needs means protecting optimal habitats, improving the wildlife-friendliness of the wider countryside, and supporting the populations of prey species.

The RSPB and other conservation bodies manage some of the UK's finest remaining habitats and have also recreated natural landscapes, creating a growing network of reserves where owls and countless other species can thrive.

But reserves alone aren't enough. Rewilding wider areas is vital, and everyone can help. Landowners and land managers – from home-owners with gardens to councils overseeing large estates – can make a difference in lots of ways, which might include creating habitat corridors, managing farmland more sustainably, and boosting biodiversity in urban spaces.

Even small changes matter. Stop using insecticides in your garden and insect numbers rise, supporting more small birds. Plant some native shrubs and their berries feed rodents like Wood Mice. More songbirds and rodents mean more food for owls. Multiply these actions across thousands of gardens and green spaces, and the result is a richer, more owl-friendly landscape.

Call to action

Hopefully, you are already an owl fan, and if so then you might also choose to be an owl ally. Owls – silent guardians of the night – lend their magic and mystique to our landscapes, and they are also key components of our diverse ecosystems. Today, their survival depends on choices we make – big and small. Here's how you can help:

Protect their homes
Get to know your local owl populations and the habitats they use, including their nest sites. You might then choose to find out who owns land where owls are hunting, roosting and breeding, and liaise

with them to ensure that the birds and their nest sites are protected from disturbance.

Bring your garden to life
A wildlife-friendly garden where insects, rodents and birds can thrive helps connect habitats together and enriches the wider countryside.

Support conservation
Join or donate to organisations like the RSPB, your local Wildlife Trust or the BTO, whose work safeguards habitats and monitors owl populations.

Spread the word
Share what you know. Encourage friends and neighbours to make small changes that add up to big results.

Celebrate owls
Enjoy their presence, learn their calls, and cherish the role they play in healthy ecosystems.

Every action counts. Together, we can ensure that the haunting beauty of an owl's call remains part of our world for generations to come.

NEST BOXES

....

Many of us know the joy of seeing a garden nest box occupied. While most gardens lack the space needed for an owl-sized box, nest box provision in the wider countryside is one of the most effective ways to support owl populations.

As noted in chapter 3, owls often struggle to find suitable nesting sites. Natural tree hollows are rare, and dead or dying trees – which provide the best cavities – are often felled as 'useless'. Even when they are left, they are fragile and eventually collapse.

For decades, farmers and rural homeowners have been encouraged to install Barn Owl boxes on their land, and today a high proportion of Barn Owl nests are in boxes rather than old buildings or tree holes. Tawny Owls also adapt readily to nest boxes, and more provision in suitable woodlands could help reverse their current decline as an Amber-listed species.

Elsewhere, nest boxes have transformed owl conservation. In Sweden, they have enabled Ural Owls to spread and thrive as a keystone species, occupying woodlands that have few natural cavities. The owls' presence supports wider biodiversity (see page 25). In Japan, nest boxes are helping Blakiston's Fish Owl recover from a near-catastrophic decline.

A well-designed nest box is more durable and sheltered than many natural cavities. It also offers practical benefits: boxes can be cleaned, repaired and monitored, and chicks can be safely removed for ringing, allowing scientists to track their future lives.

Mini Field Guide

This guide introduces the five owl species
that regularly breed in the British Isles, plus
takes a quick look at a few rare visitors.

Tawny Owl

Appearance: The largest of our owls.
Rounded and soft-looking, with a big head and
no ear tufts. Plumage is mottled brown or, more
rarely, grey; eyes are dark and relatively small.
In flight, looks front-heavy with short,
rounded wings.
Voice: The classic drawn-out, quavering, fluty
hoot of folklore – usually a male advertising his
territory. Both sexes also give a sharp two-note
ke-vick contact call, plus many
other sounds.
Where to find it:
Deciduous
woodland, parks
and large gardens
with mature trees.
Nests in tree holes, and
will use large nest boxes.

Barn Owl

Appearance: Medium-sized and slim, with a white underside and face, and golden-grey mottled upperparts. Heart-shaped facial disc; dark eyes. Flight is buoyant, with rapid wingbeats and occasional hovering.

Voice: A harsh, blood-curdling screech; also hisses and clicks.

Where to find it: Open countryside – farmland, meadows, moorland and marshes. Nests in old buildings or tree cavities.

Little Owl

Appearance: Small and compact, with a broad, flat-topped head. Grey-brown upperparts speckled white; paler underside streaked brown. Yellow eyes under pale 'eyebrows', giving a frowning look.

Voice: Sharp yelps or mewing notes, surprisingly loud for its size.

Where to find it: Farmland and open countryside with scattered mature trees. Nests in tree holes.

Long-eared Owl

Appearance: Slim, medium-sized owl with mottled grey-brown plumage tinted orange; paler below. Long ear tufts and bright orange eyes. In flight, long-winged with barred wing undersides.
Voice: Short, single hoots (lacking the quaver of Tawny Owls). Chicks beg with shrill 'squeaky-gate' calls.
Where to find it: Edges of coniferous forest and open countryside near woodland. Nests in old nests of other birds.

Short-eared Owl

Appearance: Medium-sized, sandy-grey mottled plumage; paler below. Short ear tufts and yellow eyes with black surround, giving an intense stare. In flight, long-winged with mostly pale undersides.
Voice: Series of ten or so fast, 'pumping' hoots; also harsh cat-like mews and squeals.
Where to find it: Moorland and rough grassland, including marshes (especially in winter). Nests on the ground.

RARITIES

································

These species occur as occasional visitors and/or very rare breeding birds.

Snowy Owl: Very large, mostly white with yellow eyes. Has bred in Shetland; now a very rare visitor.
Eurasian Eagle-owl: Huge, brown with orange eyes and long ear tufts. Breeds in small numbers, likely from escaped falconry birds.
Eurasian Scops Owl: Tiny, greyish owl with yellow eyes and ear tufts. Rare spring/summer visitor. Males give persistent dripping-water calls.

Further Reading and Resources

Books

Bunn, D. S., Warburton, A. B., and Wilson, R. D. S., **The Barn Owl**. 2010. T. & A. D. Poyser, London. A detailed, classic monograph on this much-loved species.

Martin, J., **The Tawny Owl**. 2022. T. & A. D. Poyser, London. A comprehensive monograph covering everything you could want to know about Tawny Owls in Eurasia.

Mikkola, H., **Owls of Europe**. 1983. T. & A. D. Poyser, London. A classic work by one of the world's leading experts, presenting species 'biographies' of Europe's owls.

Scherzinger, W., and Mebs, T., **Owls of Europe**. 2024. Christopher Helm, London. Informed by the latest research, this guide covers all aspects of European owl biology and features superb photography.

Taylor, M., **Owls**, 2013. Bloomsbury, London. Explores how owls live, followed by detailed profiles of European and North American species.

Websites

The RSPB – rspb.org.uk
The UK's leading conservation charity, dedicated to protecting wild birds and their habitats.

The Barn Owl Trust – barnowltrust.org.uk
Focused on Barn Owl study and conservation in the UK.

UK Little Owl Project – littleowlproject.uk
Research and conservation for the smallest owl species in the British Isles.

The Sound Approach – soundapproach.co.uk
Cutting-edge study of bird songs and calls.

BTO Bird Facts – bto.org/learn/about-birds/birdfacts
A one-stop resource for UK bird data – population, distribution, biometrics, survival stats and more.

Acknowledgements

Thanks to Julie Bailey for commissioning this book and others in the series. It is a great joy and privilege to write about owls once again for Bloomsbury. I am also grateful to the many researchers and scholars around the world whose work has built and continues to build on our understanding of these wonderful birds and the people, through history, who have been captivated by them. Finally, thanks to my birding and non-birding friends for useful and interesting feedback and, where needed, very welcome distraction.

Image Credits

All internal illustrations © Marianne Taylor, with the following exceptions:

P 16: (background) Romry; PP 18–19: Archiwiz/Shutterstock; P 19: (bottom) Elala/Shutterstock; P 25: (arch) Patrick Guenette/Alamy; P 36: (background) Archiwiz/Shutterstock; P 41: Trilisti/Shutterstock; P 53: Viktoria Karpunina/Shutterstock; P 59: (background) daboost/iStock; P 62: (background) Dolka/Shutterstock, (crow) ArtoPhotoDesign Studio/Shutterstock; P 69: Old Images/Alamy; PP 76–77: Topu khan/Shutterstock; PP 86–88: (background) Archiwiz/Shutterstock; P 86: Edward Lear; P 89: *The Owles Almanacke*, 1618; P 96: Küner/Alamy; P 108: (background) daboost/iStock; P 123: (background) Archiwiz/Shutterstock.

Index